Schriften des Münchner Centrums
für Governance-Forschung

herausgegeben von:

Prof. Dr. Hans-Bernd Brosius
Prof. Dr. Carsten Eckel
Prof. Dr. Edgar Grande
Prof. Dr. Carsten Reinemann
Prof. Dr. Bernhard Zangl

Band 7

Tanja A. Börzel | Jana Hönke

Security and Human Rights

Mining Companies between International Commitment and Corporate Practice

Nomos

Die Deutsche Nationalbibliothek verzeichnet diese Publikation in der Deutschen Nationalbibliografie; detaillierte bibliografische Daten sind im Internet über http://dnb.d-nb.de abrufbar.

Die Deutsche Nationalbibliothek lists this publication in the Deutsche Nationalbibliografie; detailed bibliographic data is available in the Internet at http://dnb.d-nb.de.

ISBN 978-3-8329-7740-5

1. Auflage 2012

Foreword

The rise of the global economy has drastically limited nation states' ability to regulate economic actors both within and beyond their borders. At the same time, large multinational companies increasingly commit to standards on a voluntary basis. Such standards, namely in the realm of security and human rights, are indeed becoming a key instrument in the governance toolbox. Their regulatory power, however, is difficult to evaluate. Do companies comply with such standards, regardless of their voluntary nature?

Tanja Börzel and *Jana Hönke* tackle this question in an unprecedented perspective. They analyze in particular whether multinational companies honour their commitment to the Voluntary Principles in the Democratic Republic of Congo, and they evaluate their impact on local security practices and outcomes. Complementing the 'top-down approaches' that dominate literature on voluntary programs, business and governance, both authors develop a conceptual framework from a 'bottom-up perspective', concentrating on the entire range of companies' local security practices, including their often negative effects. This allows them to evaluate corporate security practices beyond the implementation of formal programs (output) and rule-consistent behaviour (outcome). Such research leads to a more differentiated evaluation of the potential for compliance with, and the effectiveness of, voluntary standards than much of the literature on business and governance in areas of limited statehood.

The idea that voluntary, contractual standards can be an effective regulatory tool challenges many of our traditional assumptions about regulation. This makes it fitting that the present research has been presented in the "Contract Governance" lecture series here at the Munich Center on Governance, Communication, Public Policy and Law. Contract governance scholars use insights from governance theory and contract law to explore, for instance, the impact of voluntary arrangements on individual behaviour. Börzel's and Hönke's work shows that such arrangements can yield impressive results and that private self-commitment can be a very effective tool of regulation. However, their bottom-up perspective also reveals serious problems of non-compliance. As such, this perspective allows for a differentiated evaluation of voluntary arrangements that could ultimately lead to new approaches in our perennial search for regulations that avoid unnecessarily intrusive burdens and unintended consequences. For this reason, the present publication – and Contract Governance research in general – may also contribute to a better understanding of different modes of regulation.

This contribution and the “Contract Governance” lecture series in general have been made possible by generous funding of the Volkswagen Foundation. They form part of the academic activities of the respective Schumpeter research group, based at the Munich Center on Governance and at the Humboldt-University of Berlin. We are grateful to Tanja Börzel for coming to Munich and contributing this lecture.

Munich, August 2012

Florian Möslein
Schumpeter-Fellow

Abstract[1]

The Global Compact and the Voluntary Principles on Security and Human Rights increasingly commit multinational companies to human rights on a voluntary basis. Our paper investigates the security practices of multinational companies. Do they comply with voluntary human rights standards? If so, does this solve problems of increased insecurity of the local population arising from the presence of the multinational company in areas of limited statehood? We analyze in particular whether multinational companies honour their commitment to the Voluntary Principles in the Democratic Republic of Congo, and evaluate their impact on local security practices and outcomes. Our approach combines insights from the literature on compliance, governance, the sociology of rule, and critical security studies. Complementing the 'top-down approaches' that dominate literature on voluntary programs, business and governance, we develop a conceptual framework from a 'bottom-up perspective,' concentrating on the entire range of companies' local security practices, including their often negative effects. This allows us to evaluate corporate security practices beyond the implementation of formal programs (output) and rule-consistent behaviour (outcome). We do not only look for behavioural changes that can be attributed to voluntary programs but also for governance practices that may undermine or even conflict with the requirements of the Voluntary Principles. An explorative case study on two multinational mining companies in the Democratic Republic of Congo demonstrates that our approach draws a more nuanced picture of corporate security practices. Furthermore, it leads to a more differentiated evaluation of the potential for compliance with, and the effectiveness of, voluntary standards than much of the literature on business and governance in areas of limited statehood.

1 This working paper presents the findings of Jana Hönke's dissertation "Liberal Discourse and Hybrid Practise in Transnational Security Governance: Companies in Congo and South Africa in the 19th and 21st Centuries" (Hönke 2010a) as well as of the project 'Business and Governance in Sub-Saharan Africa', which is part of the Collaborative Research Center 700 "Governance in Areas of Limited Statehood, funded by the German Research Foundation (SFB 700) cf. http://www.sfb-governance.de/. We thank Miriam Weihe for her excellent research assistance, as well as Esther Thomas, Virginia Haufler and the participants of the colloquium of the Munich Center on Governance, Communication, Public Policy and Law for their helpful comments on earlier versions of the paper.

Inhaltsverzeichnis

List of abbreviations

AGA	AngloGold Ashanti
DRC	Democratic Republic of Congo
EITI	Extractive Industry Transparency Initiative
FNI	Front of National Integration
FARDC	Armed Forces of the Democratic Republic of Congo
GSF	Global Security Framework
HRW	Human Rights Watch
MNCs	Multinational Companies
OKIMO	Office of Kilo-Moto
PSC	Private Security Companies
VPs	Voluntary Principles on Security and Human Rights

1. Introduction

The Voluntary Principles on Security and Human Rights (VPs) commit multinational companies (MNC) to human rights on a voluntary basis. The governance literature has identified a credible 'shadow of hierarchy' cast by central authority as a major precondition for companies to comply with their voluntary commitments. Yet, transnational institutions, such as the VPs, not only lack enforcement capacities. The local production sites of MNCs are often hosted by states which only loosely adhere to global rights themselves and are neither willing nor capable of making non-state actors comply with them. Home states have been reluctant to foster binding regulation for the human rights behaviour of 'their' companies abroad.

Our paper investigates the security practices of MNCs and their (non-)compliance with voluntary standards in areas of limited statehood. More specifically, we analyze whether multinational mining companies operating in the Democratic Republic of Congo (DRC) honour their commitment to the Voluntary Principles on Security and Human Rights and evaluate their impact on local security practices and outcomes. Security provides a crucial case for business contributions to governance. At the same time, it points to the ambivalent role of business in zones of conflict and weak governance. On the one hand, companies seeking to protect the security of their production sights pose significant human rights challenges. Their own security agents may abuse human rights or companies may contribute to human rights abuses committed by state agencies, private security companies (PSC) or communal actors. On the other hand, companies are not only addressees of human rights norms but are also increasingly expected to act as 'norm entrepreneurs,' setting norms (Flohr et al. 2010) and enforcing them with and, if necessary, against state actors (Ruggie 2008; Deitelhoff and Wolf 2010).

Our approach combines insights from the literature on compliance, governance, the sociology of rule, and criminology. The first part of the paper develops a conceptual framework to complement the 'top-down approaches' which dominate the literature on voluntary programs, business and compliance. Instead, we advocate a 'bottom-up perspective,' placing the broad range of companies' local security practices and the various related perceptions and conflicts at the centre of our analysis. This allows us, first, to evaluate corporate security practices beyond the implementation of formal programs (output) focusing on rule-consistent behaviour (outcome). Second, we do not only look for behavioural changes that can be attributed to voluntary programs but also for governance practices that may undermine or even conflict with the requirements of the VPs. The second part of the paper presents an explorative case study on two multinational mining companies in the DRC. We demonstrate that our approach presents a more nuanced evaluation of corporate security practices and their potential compliance with voluntary standards than much of the literature on business and governance in areas of limited statehood. A bottom-up approach that takes corporate practices as a starting point reveals the limitations of transnational voluntary programs, sources of non-compliance with these programs, and contradictions between security practices of companies. The paper concludes with a discussion of avenues for future research on business and governance in areas of limited statehood.

2. Security, Human Rights and Corporate Compliance in Areas of Limited Statehood

Economic globalization has fuelled fears of a regulatory race to the bottom, in which global competition induces companies to invest in countries that lack the capacity and the willingness to set and enforce regulations, taxes and other issues affecting the costs of production (Bhagwati and Hudec 1996; Murphy 2000; Lofdahl 2002). Companies increasingly operate across national boundaries and legal jurisdictions, extending their business activities into the global South. Many developing countries lack the capacity to regulate the behaviour of transnational firms operating in their territory, or may feel hesitant to do so for fear of putting their investment at risk.

At the same time, we have seen the emergence of transnational institutions that seek to voluntarily commit multinational companies to human rights and social standards. More and more MNCs have signed up to voluntary programs, such as the UN Global Compact or the Voluntary Principles on Security and Human Rights (Flohr et al. 2010; Prakash and Potoski 2006; Ruggie 2007). Even some of the companies that have not signed up still make reference to their respect of human and social rights.

For a number of multinational companies, commitment to global social, environmental and human rights standards appears to have become less of an issue. Rather, transnational voluntary programs have been criticized for being corporate cheap talk to evade further regulation (Schäferhoff, Campe, and Kaan 2009; Brühl 2007). The lack of effective monitoring and sanctioning powers is seen as a major reason for their weakness (Flohr et al. 2010; Risse, Ropp, and Sikkink forthcoming). Like states, companies have a strong incentive to renege on their commitment if defection is unlikely to be detected and punished, particularly if they anticipate that others will not comply either. Such collective action problems at the international level are reinforced by the weak regulatory and enforcement capacities of many states that host the production sites of MNCs. Similar to transnational institutions, areas of limited statehood lack by definition the capacity to cast a credible shadow of hierarchy because governments are not capable, and often not willing, to set rights and monitor and sanction violations. So far, home states have been reluctant to impose legally binding regulation on their companies' social and human rights behaviour in other countries (Muchlinski 2007; Zerk 2006).[2] The threat to unilaterally adopt and enforce collectively binding decisions provides an important incentive for actors that are opportunistic and seek to defy the costs of cooperation and compliance (Mayntz and Scharpf 1995b). Empirical studies have confirmed the importance of such a shadow of hierarchy cast by (the threat of) state legislation for corporate self-regulation (Héritier and Lehmkuhl 2008; Börzel et al. 2011; Deitelhoff and Wolf 2010; Hamann et al. 2009).

The shadow of hierarchy and its functional equivalents

State weakness results in a serious dilemma for transnational voluntary programs in areas of limited statehood: On the one hand, the lower the capacity of the state to set and enforce rights and standards is, the greater the need becomes for transnational voluntary programs to commit MNCs to the respect of human and social rights. On the other hand, limited statehood implies a weak shadow of hierarchy. As a result, corporate compliance becomes less likely, particularly if home states and transnational institutions cannot or do not want to compensate for weak or wanting enforcement capacities at the domestic level (Börzel 2010).

The governance literature discusses the existence of functional equivalents to the shadow of hierarchy. These provide sufficient incentives for companies to ensure that companies honour their voluntary commitment and are held accountable when they seek to renege in order to maximize their individual profit. Effective equivalents to the shadow of hierarchy go beyond the threat of unilateral imposition of regulation (Deitelhoff and Wolf 2010; Börzel and Risse 2010; Börzel and Thauer forthcoming).

First, corporate compliance with voluntary standards can yield efficiency gains by enhancing the product quality and, as a consequence, the prospect of a more efficient marketing of the product (Anton, Deltas, and Khanna 2004; Parker 2002).

2 The Canadian government, for instance, has opposed binding regulations. After a long process of consultation and debate, the government opted against the recommendations of a multi-stakeholder expert group, in favour of a CSR body that has few resources and little autonomy. The US, by contrast, passed the Dodd-Frank Wall Street Reform and Consumer Protection Act in July 2010. Section 1502 requires companies whose products contain "conflict minerals", such as tin ore, coltan, wolframite and gold to disclose to the Securities and Exchange Commission (SEC) whether they are sourcing these minerals from the DRC or adjoining countries. If such conflict minerals originated in any of these countries, the manufacturing company must submit to the SEC a report describing the measures taken to avoid sourcing these minerals from armed groups in the DRC. The provisions specify that all information disclosed must be independently audited (in: http://docs.house.gov/rules/finserv/111_hr4173_finsrvcr.pdf; 5.8.2010). Global Witness celebrates the act as a step towards binding regulation on HR and 'a huge victory for corporate accountability in the oil, gas and mining industries' (Global Witness 2010). For a critique of the Act's local impact in Eastern DRC see Geenen et al. (2011).

Likewise, by incorporating environmental and social regulation into their management systems, companies have been able to secure and expand their market shares and reduce production and transaction costs (Porter and Kramer 2002; Barney 1997). Competitors may follow suit for fear of losing market shares or because they seek to emulate peers that are considered innovative and successful, particularly under conditions of high uncertainty (Bansal and Roth 2000; Potoski and Prakash 2005; Prakash and Potoski 2006). We suggest that such "California effects" (Vogel and Kagan 2004) are also at work in areas of limited statehood. Incumbent firms with high regulatory standards that are faced with a foreign competitor with low regulatory standards targeting the domestic market have an incentive to press their government to issue strict regulation to level the playing field (Börzel et al. 2011). If successful, such lobbying improves the commercial position of the forerunner firm vis-à-vis the laggard in the home market and may even force out its opponents or keep them from entering the market in the first place (Porter and van der Linde 1995; Garcia-Johnson 2000).

Corporate compliance with voluntary standards also yields efficiency gains when firms have invested substantially and with long pay-off periods – i.e., when their business model is based on "asset specificity" (Williamson 1975). Asset specificity refers in this context to intra-organizational substantial investments with a long pay off period (Thauer 2010, 2012). Such long-term investments are particularly risky in areas of limited statehood, where uncertainties are high. In situations of asset specificity, self-regulatory standards reduce the risk for uncertainty by providing an insurance of firms against potential changes in the environment (i.e. make the firm less dependent on its socio-political context).

Second, the reputation of a company and the loyalty of its clients constitute a key corporate asset (Spar and LaMure 2003). This is especially true if companies sell to the 'LOHAS' (Lifestyles of Health and Sustainability) market segment, i.e. consumers that value and demand sustainable products and the respect of social and environmental standards and are willing to pay a premium for this (Haufler 2001; Mol 2001: 97-100). While LOHAS consumers are only emerging in areas of limited statehood, companies may export to countries where they constitute a substantial share of their markets (Bansal and Roth 2000). In particular, companies with a brandname and/or products highly visible to end-consumers (Deitelhoff and Wolf 2010) will gain a competitive advantage vis-à-vis competitors if they take the lead position in their industry with respect to strict self-regulatory standards (Smith 2008; Auld, Bernstein, and Cashore 2008; Epstein 2008). Conversely, a competitor in that segment blatantly violating standards will lose customer loyalty and its reputation and, consequently, market shares (Haufler 2001; Mol 2001: 97-100; Blanton and Blanton 2007). Moreover, obvious violations of human rights or social standards may provoke campaigns by transnational NGOs (Baron 2003; Flohr et al. 2010; Newell 2001) and local community-based organizations (Eweje 2005; Lund-Thomson 2005; Bowen, Newenham-Kahindi, and Herremans 2008), particularly if companies have signed up to transnational voluntary programs, such as the Voluntary Principles on Security and Human Rights (Schepers 2006). Public shaming can result in consumer boycotts, loss of reputation and market shares, falling stock market prices and criticism by shareholders (Wheeler 2001; Hendry 2006; Waygood 2006).

Pressure on corporate compliance with voluntary standards, finally, can also emanate from peers who are concerned that 'one rotten egg spoils the entire cake', i.e. the reputation of an industry sector (Prakash 2005; Hönke forthcoming). Business associations and informal networks often act as transmitters of peer pressure (Kollman and Prakash 2001). The vulnerability of companies to these various kinds of pressures is stronger if a company has intra-firm investments in technology and human capital formation (i.e. if their business model is based on asset specific investments, Thauer 2010, 2012) or a brand name to protect, targets a high-end market, has an international (export) orientation or if its product is highly visible to end-consumers. Highly visible multinational companies operating in areas of limited statehood, such as from extractive industries for instance, are not only confronted with an alert public but also with a general suspision to do bad in these areas. Engaging in governance, even without having been targeted by a specific shaming campaign, is a way to signal good behavior to shareholders and the public (Hönke and Kranz, forthcoming).

Third, while companies operating in areas of limited statehood hardly face a credible shadow of hierarchy cast by the host state, it may be precisely the absence of the threat of strict(er) regulation that creates an incentive for companies to foster regulation. If government is not capable of adopting and enforcing collectively binding decisions, companies are not confronted with a situation in which they have to weigh the costs of cooperation and voluntary commitment against the possibility of a suboptimal hierarchically imposed policy. Rather, they face the danger of not having a common good at all. If the pursuit of their individual profit depends on the provision of certain common goods and collectively binding rules to produce them, respectively, and government is not capable or unwilling to provide them, the "shadow of anarchy" (Mayntz and Scharpf 1995a) provides companies with a major incentive to step in and fill the governance gap (Ruggie 2004; Börzel 2010), in particular when they have made asset specific investments (Thauer 2010, 2012) and therefore depend in their future operations on the investment environment they are set in. Yet, they still confront free rider problems. Hence, instead of voluntary self-regulation, collective activities in the context of business associations mitigate the free rider problem through strict rules, information provision and the imposition of costs for non-compliance (Ronit and Schneider 2000).

Fourth, while the shadow of anarchy substitutes for the shadow of hierarchy, the latter can also be generated externally. International organizations and foreign governments can commit companies to the common good. On the one hand, under international law, MNCs can be obliged to comply with standards of good governance in areas of limited statehood (Ladwig and Rudolf 2011). On the other hand, national governments of (consolidated and democratic) states, where MNCs have their headquarters, may also force them to contribute to governance in areas of limited statehood. In this particular case, home country laws are in place and enforceable which require non-state actors such as companies to comply with standards of good governance or other regulations (e.g. environmental laws) irrespective of where they invest or act. High-regulating countries are reluctant to regulate their companies outside their territory, the Alien Tort Claim Act of the US being a rare exception (Deitelhoff and Wolf 2010: 213). Yet, we know that international firms tend to transport their regulatory standards abroad as these are interpreted as 'quality signals' (Potoski and Prakash 2006) by business partners and customers (Murphy 2000; Kolk, van Tulder, and Welters 2005).

In sum, efficiency gains, reputational concerns and the absence of any state regulation may promote corporate compliance with voluntary standards. Voluntary human rights standards certainly influence reputational concerns – multinational companies that have joined the Voluntary Principles of Security and Human Rights are more vulnerable to shaming campaigns of societal actors and local communities. Human rights violations by public or company security forces can also cause significant economic costs due to local conflict disrupting the production process. At the same time, the literature finds significant variation in the compliance of companies that have joined voluntary transnational initiatives.

The local politics of compliance

Our paper argues that governance and compliance research underestimates the local conditions in which companies in areas of limited statehood operate. So called 'bottom-up' approaches in the implementation literature emphasize the resistance of local actors against compliance (Pressman and Wildavsky 1984; Hill and Hupe 2002). Yet, they neglect the competing rationalities to which actors who committed themselves to implementation are subject (Hönke forthcoming; Höppner and Nagl 2008). For instance, case studies on oil companies in the Niger Delta demonstrate how corporate social responsibility discourse and engagement with communities are part and parcel of the local conflict system. In many cases, strategic philanthropy becomes part of companies' security management *vis-à-vis* community conflict, alongside deterrence and surveillance approaches (Zalik 2004; Frynas

2000). Also, multinational companies collaborate with host governments and try to comply with their expectations, which are often different from these standards (Reno 2001). The rentier literature directs attention to such structural power and the effects of transnational mining companies on governance to strengthen autocratic governments. Governments in many cases still act as the main gatekeeper between the domestic and the international spheres (Reno 2001; Bayart 1993: 198). In spite of their overall weak capacities, governments retain the monopoly over symbolic capital and make decisions regarding mining rights. New modes of governance thus interact with other transnational and local modes of governance in areas of limited statehood (Hönke forthcoming).

Understanding the role of companies in local governance in areas of limited statehood, and more specifically, questioning if and how their commitment to voluntary human rights standards impacts local security practices and outcomes, requires a different perspective on voluntary standards than we often find in the literature. We need to take actual corporate practices as a starting point. Rather than merely focusing on evidence for compliance and effective program implementation, we should also analyse corporate security practices – compliant *and* non-compliant – and consider their effects on collective security at the local level. Instead of selecting only cases of successful corporate engagement, this implies focusing on the broader range of governance practices, which might undermine or even conflict with the requirements of transnational programs.

As an important first step towards re-evaluating corporate compliance with transnational voluntary standards, our paper develops an analytical framework that allows for a more balanced mapping of companies' security practices beyond the formal implementation of transnational voluntary programs. This not only enables us to explore to what extent MNCs operating in areas of limited statehood comply with transnational voluntary programs, such as the VPs. We also go beyond compliance to understand the broader range of parallel and often competing security practices that companies apply at their production sites (see also Hönke forthcoming).

3. Studying Corporate Security Practices Top-down and Bottom-up

A top-down approach to corporate security practices focuses on the compliance of companies with voluntary human rights standards. Compliance is usually defined as rule-consistent behaviour (cf. Raustiala and Slaughter 2002). Consequently, MNCs are required to implement transnational voluntary programs by (1) incorporating transnational principles and standards into their corporate regulations to amend and repeal conflicting rules, and (2) integrating them into their management systems by setting up the administrative infrastructure and resources necessary to put them into practice, to monitor rule-consistent behaviour, and to sanction violations (Danish Institute for Human Rights 2006). While these *output*-related activities are important, MNCs have to make the necessary changes in their governance practices to make their behaviour consistent with the requirements of transnational principles and standards, and to refrain from action which violates them (cf. Deitelhoff and Wolf 2010: 14-15). Many studies point to the decoupling of actual behaviour from institutional changes (e.g. Flohr et al. 2010) or neglect the *outcome* dimension entirely, which provides an important, though not singular, link between the implementation of transnational programs and the solution of the problems they address. While their *effectiveness* does not exclusively depend on the rule-consistent behaviour of companies (after all, the principles and standards could be ill-defined to address rights violations in the first place, or companies could be a lesser part of the problem than assumed), corporate compliance should help improve the rights situation.

Therefore, we identify three analytical steps for compliance studies to evaluate company practices on the ground:

Step 1 – *Transnational demand*: Identify the requirements defined by the voluntary principles and standards, with regard to both procedures and substance. What do they expect companies to do and not to do?

Step 2 – *Company output*: Trace the incorporation of these requirements into corporate rules and management systems and the service agreements with contractors. Does the company make explicit reference to the voluntary program? Do the voluntary principles and standards form part of its corporate identity? Have there been any changes after the establishment of official commitment to the transnational voluntary program? Have new responsibilities, procedures and resources (human, financial, technical) been introduced (e.g. in the internal auditing system) to put the principles and standards into practice, to monitor compliance, and to sanction violations, also 'down the supply chain'?

Step 3 – *Company outcome*: Assess the changes in company practices necessitated by the voluntary principles and standards and the company's output. Has the company taken the necessary action to make the behaviour of its employees and contractors consistent with the transnational requirements and the stipulations of corporate institutions and policies? Are new policies put into practice? Is the money spent? Is new personnel employed and old personnel retrained? Is rule-consistent behaviour rewarded and non-compliance punished?

Still, tracing both the output and outcome of MNCs with regard to voluntary programs only provides a partial and at times distorted picture of corporate security practices and their effects on human rights and security in host communities. Corporate governance practices that are not directly related to voluntary programs may undermine or even conflict with these programs' requirements, and negatively affect the security and human rights of local communities. Such business practices tend to be overlooked by a top-down perspective. Therefore, we not only assess to what extent the behaviour of MNCs complies with the VPs, but also examine a broader range of companies' security practices and potential contradictions and conflict between them.

A bottom-up perspective allows us to direct attention to the entirety of local security practices by companies (Hönke forthcoming). Drawing on practice approaches in security studies (Leander 2010) and research on plural policing in criminology (Johnston and Shearing 2003), corporate security practices can be understood as the routinised and institutionalized words and actions of company agents seeking to secure operations on a daily basis. Security practices denote what company agents or members of local communities refer to as 'security issues.' One would first ask what local company agents identify as security issues. The issues addressed in the transnational regulation and in company programs may substantially differ from the everyday understanding of local management and security staff. What do local people perceive as potential factors of insecurity? Second, one would ask how the security problems identified by a company are being addressed on a day-to-day basis. Just as mining firms, for instance, usually combine different reactive and preventive strategies, security practices may range from fencing off parts of a concession area and putting it under surveillance, to co-opting local chiefs, to social investment in local communities. Finally, beyond compliance or non-compliance with the VPs, what are the (unintended) effects of company security practices (Hönke forthcoming; also Hönke, with Thomas 2012)?

Three analytical steps can be identified for analyzing transnational voluntary principles and corporate security practices in the local arena:

Step 1 – *Perceptions of security issues*: Analyze the issues identified as security problems by local company agents, the VPs, and by people living in the vicinity of mining operations. Look at the issues that are not understood to be security problems. What is established as a problem of (in)security, and how are areas of responsibility defined?

Step 2 – *Routine security practices*: Map how companies and other agents they work with, such as Private Security Companies (PSCs) or local chiefs, address these security issues in their day-to-day practices. What do they actually do? By which means do companies attempt to provide security? What is the scope of security measures? In other words, how inclusively do companies aim to provide security (for whom/where)? Who is targeted, excluded or otherwise affected by these measures?

Step 3 –*Unintended effects, competing norms and discourses* – What explains non-compliant practices? How can we understand the hybrid mix of corporate security practices at the local level and the contradictions attached to corporate governance interventions? What role do the VPs play and what do they omit from the companies' security/human rights agenda?

To illustrate our argument and demonstrate the added value of a bottom-up research design, we conduct two exploratory case studies of the corporate security practices of two mining companies in the DRC, examining their compliance with the Voluntary Principles on Security and Human Rights and their effects on collective security at the local level.

4. Mining companies' security practices and the Voluntary Principles on Security and Human Rights in the DRC

Since the 1990s, the extractive industry increasingly operates in areas of weak governance and conflict zones where the allocation of resources and property rights are highly contested, and state security forces often produce insecurity and violate human rights. Companies seeking to protect their property or extract private benefit from the mine and from the local population often cause violent conflicts at the local level. Artisanal mining poses a particular challenge to MNCs: There is an inherent potential for conflict between large-scale operators and small-scale miners who work on the land licensed to the company, but claim to have an historical entitlement. In addition to access to mineral resources, land, and resettlement, the redistribution of economic benefits is often contested. Potential conflict is exacerbated by the lack of (enforced) regulation or by ambiguous legislation that does not take into account the concerns of artisanal operators and local populations, extending conflict to company security forces (Hönke 2010b).[3] A series of industry-community conflicts and accidents over the last decade has seriously damaged the reputation of the extractive industry, in particular since critics have increasingly gained attention in international politics (Szablowski 2007).

The VPs are the only transnational human rights guidelines directed specifically to oil, gas and mining companies, which face particular problems in balancing security concerns with the respect for human rights and fundamental freedoms, and which have faced particularly strong criticism for (complicity with) human rights abuses. The non-binding VPs were established in 2000 as a response to several incidents of human rights violations by security forces seeking to protect oil and mining installations of MNCs with headquarters in the UK and the US. The initiative came from the UK and US governments in order to ensure the operation of their key oil companies in Indonesia, Columbia and Nigeria at the time, and were thus jointly developed with seven major Anglo-American extraction companies and human rights NGOs (Freeman 2002; Hansen 2009). While the VPs were created before the Extractive Industry Transparency Initiative (EITI) and the Kimberley Process Certification Scheme, the VPs have gained less recognition. To date, they may be the most comprehensive and specific standard with regard to private business and human rights (Freeman and Hernandez Uriz 2003).

3 The 2002 DRC Mining Code, for instance, prohibits small-scale mining on concessions which have been licensed to larger mining companies, even though it is the only viable source of income for many people.

Yet, the VPs are not very specific, hardly monitored or enforced, and face many problems with implementation, and it remains to be seen if that will change significantly in the future (Freeman 2005; Ruggie 2010). The VP governance institutions lack centralized monitoring and sanctioning powers, which reflects the dominant interest coalition of business and government and their preference for soft regulation. For this reason, Global Witness, the leading INGO in the area of resource extraction, security, and human rights, did not take part in the VP process, and Safer World left the Initiative in 2007 (Global Witness 2007; Freeman 2005). In 2007, formal participation criteria were adopted for the first time. The participation criteria also detail provisions for the expulsion of participants that fail to comply with the VPs. This, however, requires a unanimous decision by all members. Participants may also raise concerns regarding whether other participants have met the VP criteria or show a sustained lack of effort to implement the VPs (The Voluntary Principles 2009). The VP dispute resolution process was used for the first time by Oxfam in 2009, criticizing Newmont for its security and human rights practices. Newmont agreed to an independent review (VPs 2010a: 2). Some MNCs are also pushing forward with the implementation of the VPs, despite the low degree of legalisation, which may improve the VPs impact in the future.

Limited membership raises another problem for the VPs. The VPs had initially been confined to the US and UK governments and seven US and UK companies. 10 additional extractive companies have become members,[4] which include some major MNCs. Yet, corporate membership remains confined to Northern Europe and North America. In that same year, the organization removed a requirement that companies or NGOs could only participate in the plenary if their home governments were also participants, which paved the way toward an expansion of the Voluntary Principles membership. And while only seven out of the top 25 international metal mining companies joined the initiative (UNCTAD 2007), less visible small and medium-sized companies, in particular in exploration and trade, are not represented at all. This is also true for the governments involved. Five other governments have joined the initiative: the Netherlands in 2001, Norway in 2003 and Switzerland, Canada and Colombia this year, the latter being the only host country of MNCs that has joined the VPs so far. Important European countries, such as France or Germany, have declined to participate, as have all of the new major home countries for investors in oil and mining in Africa and elsewhere, such as Brazil, India, Russia, South Africa and China.

4 Current members are AngloGold Ashanti, Anglo American, the BG Group, BHP Billiton, BP, Chevron, Conoco Phillips, Exxon Mobil, Freeport McMoRan Copper and Gold, Hess Corporation, Marathon Oil, Newmont Mining Corporation, Occidental Petroleum Corporation, Rio Tinto, Shell, Statoil, and Talisman Energy (VPs 2010b).

Due to the limited data available and accessible, there are hardly any studies on corporate compliance with the VPs. The few that exist are either not fully independent of the company studied (Jim Freedman Consulting 2006; Kapelus 2006), limit themselves to an analysis of company policies (output) (Hofferberth 2010), focus mostly on the politics behind the VPs and the resulting lack of clarity and accountability of the principles themselves (Hansen 2009), or use sporadic evidence from different companies and places (Global Witness 2007a). There are a few studies on company security practices at the local level, yet most of them do not systematically discuss the direct and indirect effects of the VPs on local security practices (Zalik 2004; Frynas 2000). Ultimately, both compliance and corporate security practices in a broader sense can only be assessed at the level of individual company operations.

The next section will demonstrate the limitations of a top-down compliance perspective and the added value of a bottom-up approach, focusing on corporate practices at two mining sites of two major mining companies in the DRC: AngloGold Ashanti (AGA) and Anvil Mining. Both have been subject to international human rights campaigns, resulting in their comparatively strong commitment to implementing the VPs. Although AGA and Anvil differ in size, their activities are of similar importance to the DRC. The governments of their home countries (South Africa and Australia) are not members of the VPs. Nor do the two MNCs belong to the group of the 'most likely cases' of North American and European firms, which are the leaders in integrating human rights into their management systems (Hamann et al. 2009: 455-456). Finally, AGA and Anvil are mining companies which, unlike oil firms, have not received much attention in the literature.

AGA was founded in 2004 as a merger of Ghanaian Ashanti Goldfields Company Limited and South African AngloGold Limited. It is the third largest gold mining company in the world with 21 operations across four continents. Listed on 8 stock exchanges and employing 63,364 people in 2009, the company is headquartered in South Africa (AngloGold Ashanti 2009a). AGA invested in the parastatal gold company Office of Kilo-Moto (OKIMO) and gained shares in a 10,000km^2 concession situated in the remote north eastern Ituri area. The MNC is concentrated around the city of Mongbwalu, close to the Ugandan border. In 1996, it began detailed explorations, the same year in which the cross-border conflict between warring militias and government forces began. AGA left its exploration site in Mongbwalu in 2002 when the war made mining impossible. One year later, AGA returned and entered talks with the Front of National Integration (FNI), an armed militia linked to Uganda, which controlled Mongbwalu at the time. The financial and other support AGA gave to the FNI in 2004 in return for allowing its exploration activities to resume in Mongbwalu, in the same year it joined the Global

Compact,[5] gave rise to significant pressure by the human rights community (HRW 2005) and fuelled the debate on the role of business in conflict and weak governance zones (Kapelus, Hamann, and O'Keefe 2008). In 2005, AGA publicly renounced its financial support of FNI in the DRC as a regrettable mistake and a breach of its principles and values, but pledged to continue its exploration program (AGA 2005). In 2007, AGA became a member of the VPs. A report by Human Rights Watch of 2005 denouncing the activities of AGA in the DRC claimed that the VPs would have helped the company to make the right decisions on when and under which circumstances to start operations in Mongbwalu (HRW 2005).

Anvil Mining was a medium-sized Australian company that had several mining operations in the DRC and was listed at the Toronto stock exchange. Anvil Mining was recently purchased by Minmetals Resources, a subsidiary of the Chinese state-owned Minmetals Group, in February 2012.[6] However, when we did our fieldwork for this paper, Anvil was one of the major Western companies in industrial mining in the Copperbelt in Southern Katanga, one of the most important mining areas in the DRC (see Anvil Mining 2008a, 2011). In 2004, Anvil was involved in human rights abuses carried out by the Congolese army (FARDC) near its Dikulushi Mine. During its attempt to recapture the town of Kilwa, serious human rights violations occurred, such as summary executions of rebels. Congolese soldiers also used Anvil's vehicles to transport looted goods and corpses. Moreover, the airplanes which Anvil had chartered to evacuate its employees were used for troop transports. Anvil admitted that it had provided food, tents, and pay to Congolese soldiers during the operation. In the military prosecution of war crimes, three of Anvil's employees were charged with aiding and abetting the FARDC in committing crimes in 2006 (Global Witness 2007b). The Congolese military court did find Anvil and its employees not guilty in 2007. Yet, the case received considerable international attention and put Anvil under sustained pressure from human rights groups who did not accept the court ruling due to its lack of independence.[7] In response to these events the company did not formally join the VPs, yet committed itself to applying these security principles in practice.

While sharing a number of similarities, AGA and Anvil show some important differences, which should increase the capacity to generalize our findings. While gold miner AGA has been in the exploration phase in Mongbwalu and Kibali in the DRC since 1996, Anvil gained its first contract as early as 1998 and produced

5 The first two of the ten principles of the Global Compact require businesses to support and respect the protection of internationally proclaimed human rights, and to make sure that they are not complicit in human rights abuses (UN Global Compact 2006).

6 Hook. Leslie: Minmetals wins Anvil Mining for C$1.3bn, Financial Times 17 February 2012, http://www.ft.com/cms/s/0/9f85e210-5960-11e1-abf1-00144feabdc0.html#axzz2036S9XFd [last accessed July 10 2012].

7 Interviews with Pact Congo and ACIDH, October 2008, Lubumbashi.

copper and cobalt from the DRC since 2002 (Ministère des Mines 2007). Moreover, Anvil operated in the relatively stable Katanga province, which had been controlled by the Kabila governments throughout the Congolese wars. The Ituri Province, where AGA works, is still conflict-ridden and government has little control. Analyzing the security practices and their compliance with the VPs of the two companies will provide us with a sufficiently broad empirical basis for probing the added value of our analytical framework.

In the following sections, we will evaluate to what extent AGA and Anvil have honoured their commitments and complied with the VPs, and will discuss the results in light of the broader range of corporate security practices. Our empirical analysis is based on documents provided on the websites of VPs, AGA, and Anvil, as well as human rights NGOs that have been active in the DRC. If available, we have also consulted annual reports, business principles, country reports, case studies on human rights, and specific site reports. Additionally, we draw on extensive field observations and interviews conducted in the DRC.

4.1 Companies and security governance: Top-Down

While remaining rather unspecific and hardly institutionalised, the VPs provide an operational approach for companies to identify human rights and security risk, as well as to improve the human rights record of their security agents by engaging and collaborating with state and private security forces on these issues (VPs 2011a). They are divided into three sections covering the internal management system of the company and its external relations with public and private security forces.

Transnational demand

While the VPs themselves are rather broadly defined, guidelines provide some indication of what companies are expected to do in the implementation (VPs a).[8] First, companies shall integrate the VPs into their management systems, contracts and agreements, preferably prior to starting an operation. This includes most importantly putting a specific human rights policy in place and conducting regular risk and impact assessments based on extensive background information on various criteria (e.g. causes and potentials for local conflict, human rights records of security forces and law enforcement officers, and the rule of law performance of do-

8 An implementation guidance tool was published by World Bank MIGA in cooperation with Anvil Mining in 2008. Its update and increased use is on the agenda for the next five years (VPs 2010a).

mestic institutions) drawn from and shared with a wide variety of actors, including local and national governments, security firms, other companies, home governments, multilateral institutions, and civil society (VPs 2011b). Compliance requires companies to adopt a human rights policy and adapt their risk assessments to the criteria stipulated by the VPs, develop performance indicators and guidelines for risk and impact assessments (output), and conduct them accordingly (outcome). They may also embed the VPs in their annual performance reviews, develop implementation manuals and training materials (output), and organize implementation workshops and training programs for their employees (and their security contractors, see below) (outcome). Finally, companies shall set-up communication channels (output) and use them (outcome) to share risk assessment information and report human rights violations inside and outside the company.

Second, companies shall help ensure that actions of governments and public security providers are consistent with the protection and promotion of human rights (VPs 2011c). This involves making corporate security policies transparent to the public security providers and the public, particularly with regard to the "ethical principles" they are based upon. In addition to engaging public security forces into a regular dialogue on the importance of human rights, companies shall engage in capacity-building by supporting human rights training and education for public security forces, and helping to strengthen state institutions to ensure accountability and respect for human rights. Except for the provision of equipment, no further reference is made to how exactly companies shall engage in human rights capacity- and institution-building. Finally, companies shall report any human rights violations and support state investigations. While remaining rather vague, compliance with the VPs on public security asks companies to clearly state their security policy and make it publicly available, and to establish common communication channels and policies (responsibilities, personnel, time, money) with governments, public security forces, civil society, local communities, and other companies on human rights issues. These policies should particularly represent responses to human rights violations (e.g. whistle-blower protection). At the same time, they should provide technical and financial assistance to train public security forces and state authorities on respecting human rights (output) and to actively engage in consultation and capacity-building accordingly (outcome).

Third, companies that enlist the assistance of private security companies (PSC) because the host country is not willing or capable to protect the company's production site shall make sure that the PSCs comply with international and national human rights standards (VPs 2011d). Using their contractual relationships, companies shall act as enforcement authorities committing PSCs to human rights, monitoring their compliance and sanctioning violations, e.g. by blacklisting. To comply with the VPs on private security, MNCs must only contract private security companies, if governments are unable or unwilling to provide sufficient public security (outcome). Moreover, companies should have a policy to only contract PSCs that have a clear human rights policy, a clean human rights record, adequately trained personnel (output), and no business relations with PSCs that do not fulfil these requirements (outcome). Companies should conduct human rights screening, make background checks, and consult with other companies, home country officials, host country officials, and civil society regarding experiences with private security (outcome). Finally, companies must have a human rights clause, put procedures in place to monitor and sanction the human rights behaviour of their contractors, develop HR training programs (output), and use them accordingly (outcome).

However, guidance for effective implementation remains limited. An in-country implementation process involving representatives from participant companies, the host government, civil society and local communities shall support compliance with the VPs by helping to formally integrate them into host country policies and practices, and by facilitating dialogue between private, public, and civil sectors around human rights and security practices (VPs b). Yet, such in-country implementation processes are still the exception (VPs a). With the exception of Colombia, lack of engagement by home states and the initiative itself with host governments seems the major impediment for effective implementation (Freeman 2005: 4).

There is also a range of reporting requirements. Participants shall prepare and submit to the steering committee, one month prior to the Annual Plenary Meeting of VP, a report on their efforts to implement or to assist in the implementation of VPs. The Reporting Working Group drafted reporting guidelines, which were used as a basis for the 2010 reports for the first time (VPs a). In 2007, formal participation criteria were adopted for the first time. In that same year, the requirement that companies or NGOs could participate in the Plenary only if their home governments were also participants was removed, which paved the way toward an expansion of the Voluntary Principles membership. With the amendment of the criteria in 2009, the 'fractious issue of participation criteria for governments' was finally resolved and interim reporting criteria were agreed upon (Freeman 2010). Participants are now required to publicly report on the implementation of the VPs or on their support of implementation. The participation criteria now also include provisions for the expulsion of participants. Participants may even raise concerns regarding non-compliant behaviour by other participants (VPs a). While the members of VP seek to make requirements more precise, VP reports, files and proceedings remain non-public.

Company output

The VPs are rather vague as to what they expect companies to do, and do not specify how companies should fulfil these expectations. This renders a compliance evaluation difficult. Also, the lack of an internal auditing system that provides for an independent verification of whether VPs are put into practice further undermines the effectiveness of the voluntary program (VPs a).[9]

AGA includes a statement on the VPs on its website. However, it is very general and not integrated in the "Corporate governance and policies." The latter refers to obligations in terms of the US Sarbanes-Oxley Act of 2002, NYSE and JSE Rules, and the King Report on Corporate Governance 2002, and does not include the VPs; the obligations cover health, safety, environment, and community standards, but do not mention human rights. Anvil, by contrast, adopted a "Code of Business Conduct" in 2007, which prominently features human rights, including a section on security and human rights, which commits Anvil to observing "the principles set out in the Voluntary Principles on Security and Human Rights in relation to security, risk assessment and the maintenance of human rights" (Anvil Mining 2007: 11). Moreover, Anvil's Corporate Social Responsibility refer to the VPs as part of the company's commitment to the "highest standards of corporate governance, ethical behaviour, and respect for human rights" (Anvil 2008).

AGA claims that its Environment and Community Affairs Committee develops company policy and guidelines "to assist operations in acting in accordance with the group's business principles and policies," which should include human rights. There have also been plans for the conduct of a company-wide security review in 2008 (AGA a). Equally broad is the reference to a new Global Security Framework (GSF) developed by the newly established Global Security Department in 2008, headed by the Global Security Vice President and progressively implemented since 2009 (AGA a). The GSF's nine key processes include "Voluntary Principles, Policy Standards and Compliance" (AGA 2009b). Procedures, standards and best practices have been set-up and constantly reviewed with the help of self-audits to ensure compliance (AGA 2009b). They include a code of conduct, operational standards, a risk assessment toolkit, and accompanying guidelines (AGA 2008: 5). The annual performance report explicitly addresses human rights and refers to the VPs as part of AGA's global security framework. The Sustainability Reviews also specify performance criteria on human rights, such as human rights clauses and human rights screening of investment agreements, human rights screening of suppliers and contractors in the application process, employee and security personnel training on policies, and procedure concerning aspects of human rights (AGA 2009c). Next to

9 See UNSG SR John Ruggie's call for more engagement in his plenary address to the VP meeting 2010 (Ruggie 2010).

the Sustainability Reviews (AGA 2009d; AGA a), AGA has issued Annual Voluntary Principle Reports since 2008 that broadly outline its human rights policies and procedures (AGA b).

Similar to AGA, Anvil initiated a comprehensive implementation project to imbed the VPs in the corporate culture and management system. Together with the Multilateral Investment Guarantee Agency of the World Bank, Anvil funded a diagnostic study by a consultant that developed a VP implementation program for Anvil's operations in Africa, including an implementation toolkit for a mining company operating in a post-conflict African country (World Bank Group 2008). The toolkit provides a detailed manual on how to systematically put the VPs into practice, including a time-phased implementation plan. Moreover, Pact Congo, an American developmental NGO, drafted a Framework on Security and Human Rights on Anvil's request, which guides the company's incorporation of human rights into its security program (Jim Freedman Counsulting 2006). Like AGA, the company issues annual Sustainability Reports, which have a short section on risk assessment that also makes reference to the VPs. However, no details are given and the last report available on the website was from 2007. While risk assessments procedures appear to exist in both companies, there is no information on whether VP criteria are taken into consideration. AGA has developed an internal audit system with a VP checklist to review progress on implementing the VPs at local facilities. This will be integrated into the ISO 14001 management system, along with the incorporation of community standards (AGA a). Equally unavailable is specific information on human rights screening, training of public security forces and private security companies, which are enlisted for protection of its production sites (AGA a: 2, 5). In conflict zones such as the DRC, AGA and Anvil both employ public and private security forces. AGA justifies its reliance on "fee for services" support by the police, the army, and private security companies (AGA 2008: 1) on the basis of threat and risk assessments which indicate that security threats are "sufficiently elevated" (AGA 2009b: 2). Both companies have developed programs to communicate with and train staff, and incorporate the VPs into contracts with public and private service providers. Procedures have been introduced to report and investigate security-related incidents with human rights implications by public/ private security forces deriving from the company's activities (Jim Freedman Consulting 2006).

Finally, AGA claims to have recently established a government relations function in order to give public policy strategy a greater focus in the business. It has also developed an engagement strategy for government and a management standard related to engagement with stakeholders, to be introduced across all its operations in 2010 (AGA a: 5). Again, no specific information is available. In a similar vein, Anvil and the government of Katanga have signed a Protocol to govern the interaction between Anvil and the Province of Katanga (Jim Freedman Consulting 2006). To what extent this Protocol provides for communication channels on human rights issues is unclear.

Overall, AGA and Anvil appear to have incorporated the VPs into their corporate policies, management systems and agreements with service providers. The VPs are explicitly referred to and form part of the companies' corporate identity. Both companies have introduced substantial changes to their management policies and procedures including the dedication of human, financial and technical resources. While the Global Compact also includes human rights principles, human rights only gained prominence after AGA joined the VPs in 2007, even though they feature less prominently than other standards (so far). Anvil, too, only started to develop a human rights policy based on the VPs after it had been subjected to an international campaign, even though it did not become an official member of VPs. At the same time, it is difficult to assess the comprehensiveness of the related changes in the corporate policies and management systems of the two companies, given that AGA and Anvil provide rather general information on the measures and actions taken.

Company outcome

Unlike Anvil, AGA annually reports on its implementation of the VPs to shareholders through its Annual Financial Statements, and to all stakeholders through its VP Reports and the corporate social responsibility report. The company states, for instance, that in 2009 86% of AGA's employees and security personnel received human rights training (AGA 2009c). The reports also mention that AGA's security departments engage in self-reporting to the company, local authorities and local communities regarding human rights violations by employees, contractors and public security forces (AGA 2009b: 2). Such incidents are documented in the annual VP Reports. There is, however, no external review of this information. Anvil, by contrast, does not report on these issues. However, the company participates in and prominently supports the Katanga security forum, in which representatives of large mining companies, state security forces, the UN mission MONUC and others discuss security and potentially also human rights issues, and exchange information on incidents of human rights abuses.[10]

AGA claims to conduct risk and impact assessments in the DRC, e.g. to decide whether to enlist the service of public and private security forces (AGA 2009b: 2). To what extent these assessments apply the VPs is unclear. Anvil has not conducted

10 Interview with Pact Congo representatives, October 17 and November 6 2008, Lubumbashi; see further discussion in Hönke (2010: 224f).

risk assessments on its own (Jim Freedman Consulting 2006). With regard to integrating human rights into contracts with public and private security forces, AGA announced a general review of all contracts on the basis of a contractor vetting checklist, as well as the standardization of contract requirements with service providers in 2010. This includes briefing government officials on human rights, as well as training public and private security forces, personnel employed by contractors, members of the police and military, community groups, and civil society organizations on the company's human rights policies and the VPs (AGA a: 3, 5-6). While Anvil's own security personnel is well trained and informed, neither the private security company, Securicor, nor the local police and Mine Police that Securicor works with seem to have received any substantial training on human rights (Jim Freedman Consulting 2006). Anvil, however, tried to get government approval for human rights training for Mine Police forces through contracted NGO Pact Congo.

Finally, both companies have sought to set up communication channels in neighbouring settlements for discussions with the local communities (Jim Freedman Consulting 2006). It remains unclear to what extent they engage in human rights dialogues with local authorities, local communities or civil society. AGA does not seem to have established any regular contact or information sharing with the local communities. In 2006, it had set up the Mongbwalu Forum of Stakeholders, which, however, is not used for advancing VPs. It is not part of the Ituri Stakeholder Forum in the provincial capital Bunia, which organizes important NGOs and social groups. Working closely with INGOs, HRW and Pax Christi, the forum has remained highly critical of AGA's social and human rights policies and impact.[11] While it has apparently conducted a risk assessment, AGA has not published a human rights or any other assessment for the Mongbwalu project that includes the participation of affected communities (CAFOD 2010). To what extent AGA has used the renegotiation of its mining contract with the DRC government to communicate its human rights policy and to engage the government in a human rights dialogue is questionable as well.[12]

Overall, available information renders it extremely difficult to assess the behavioural compliance of AGA and Anvil with the VPs. Implementation only started in 2008 and 2007, respectively, and many changes had just been introduced when we conducted our research.

11 Interview with manager community relations and social development, AGA, 3 October 2007, Johannesburg.

12 In 2007, the DRC government embarked on a review of over 60 mining contracts signed between 1996 and 2003 during the Congolese war, including the contract with AGA.

4.2 Companies and security governance – Bottom-up

The top-town analysis of company security practices above takes a voluntary program, such as the VPs, and examines to what extent company policies and practices comply with them. In the following, we demonstrate how a bottom-up approach focusing on local practices re-evaluates the VPs and corporate governance contributions and broadens our understanding of business in local governance.[13] We aim to overcome two limitations of the top-down perspective. First, top-down studies tend to emphasize (transnational) policy formulation and politics, resulting in a narrow view of the actual security practices of MNCs at their production sites and a neglect of local discourse and politics. Second, focusing on corporate governance contributions as defined by the VPs omits from the analysis other everyday security practices employed by MNCs. By using a particular transnational standard, such as the VPs, as a yardstick to assess company behaviour, it is easy to neglect competing understandings and expectations of what should be considered security and human rights issues in the local arena, and who should care about them. It is important in this regard to remember that the VPs emerged as a minimal consensus between two governments, a small number of extractive MNCs opposing strict regulation, and a few NGOs.

A bottom-up perspective starts from the other side. We analyse in the following local, everyday security practices of the two mining companies, as well as the accompanying conflicts and contradictory understandings of security and rights. This new focus improves our assessment of transnational voluntary programs and enhances our understanding of non-compliance and security practices that follow different and often competing norms. The following is based on research on AGA and Anvil that was conducted between 2007 and 2010.

Perceptions of security – defining and scoping an issue

Anvil's and AGA's security managers share a narrow understanding of security as the protection of property and personnel against threats from intruders. Their concern is security as a private good. They list "illegal mining" and theft among the most serious security challenges faced by their companies in the DRC. In the eyes of the security department of Anvil, the company is threatened by organized groups, members of the local communities, and its own workers. Cobalt, copper cable, cement, petrol and equipment are among the disappearing goods. In particular, thousands of artisanal miners infiltrate Anvil's concessions and are described as a

13 For a more in-depth treatment of the approach see Hönke (2010a: 49-74) and Hönke (2012, forthcoming).

major security risk.[14] While petty theft seems to be less an issue in the smaller exploration sites around Mongbwalu, AGA, too, identifies artisanal miners who 'illegally' mine gold on their concession as major security risk. There are more than 100,000 small-scale miners in the gold mining area, many of them former militias with strong political allegiances in the area (Kapelus et al. 2008: 127).

Like other mining companies in the DRC, Anvil's local managers believe that security risks increasingly emanate from the society and local communities in which they operate. Mining sites – e.g. on-shore oil operations such as those in the Niger Delta – cannot be fenced off easily from the social and political conflicts in which they operate and which they partly cause (Hönke 2010a: 169; Szablowski 2007: 27-60). While the situation in Ituri is more volatile, in both areas companies operate in a complex social and political context characterized by the legacy of war and divided by political factions, in which mining companies are part of popular memories of warfare, suffering, and political conflict (Kapelus, Hamann, and O'Keefe 2008; Hönke 2010b). Reputational risks related to social and security issues have grown over recent years. Incidents such as community protest and violence of security forces against the population are now seen by some firms as security issues, in the sense that they may negatively impact shareholder value, profits and contracts.[15]

The VPs do not question this framing of company security concerns. Having been developed by governments and companies favouring economic liberalism, they start from the assumption that, first, companies' legal title and property rights needed to be defended, and second, that the business of business was essentially doing business. Yet companies should at least reduce negative externalities, such as harming the human rights of others with their daily security practices. In this context the VPs provide some guidelines for reducing the negative effects of corporate private protection measures on communities. They do not, however, require companies to provide security for others at the local level. Asking them to teach human rights to state security agents may contribute to better security provision for the broader local public; however, companies' willingness and ability to influence the local police or military are limited in this regard. Also, specific local measures

14 Interview with company security manager DRC, Anvil Mining, 22 November 2008, Lubumbashi.

15 The International Council of Mines and Metals, a transnational business association representing a number of large MNCs from the mining industry in public relations issues in the area of sustainable development, started explicitly recognising problems related to corporate security practices as an issue in 2003. Since 2005, the association engages with the UNSRSG special representative John Ruggie, and has published guidelines that shall help member companies in managing human rights and security-related issues (in: http://www.icmm.com /page/225/business-and-human-rights; 6 August.2010). Concerning companies in the DRC and Anvil in particular: Interview with security and VP managers, Anvil Mining, October 2008, Lubumbashi, Interviews with Pact Congo 17 October and 6 November 2008, Lubumbashi.

are countered by companies financing and strengthening an unreliable and repressive regime and its security forces in the DRC (see below).

Second, the VPs are largely oblivious to the concerns of the people living in the areas in which these mining companies intervene. Insecurity and conflicts evolve around the highly contested question of who has legitimate access to resources, of who shall have access to land, and who has to bear the costs of mining. To artisanal miners who used to work on Anvil Mining's concession, the company's claim to the resources is illegitimate because it is based on a questionable contract with a distant government in Kinshasa. As they reclaim their right to make a living from 'their resources,' local community members demand the redistribution of company profits to them in order to provide social security (Hönke, 2010a: 201-228). Both point to the important underlying struggle over how the access to and the benefits from extraction should be distributed. Investment in industrial mining in the DRC might not bring many changes for the political networks that are in power, but could alter the ways in which they benefit from resource extraction. For competing political networks and in particular for the local population and migrants who make up the large artisanal mining community, mining activities of MNCs change everything and often put their source of income at risk (Hönke 2010b).

Third, and related to the previous points, the VPs are insensitive to the governance expectations in areas of limited statehood. Both AGA and Anvil face huge expectations and demands for social benefits. In the context of a state that does not redistribute wealth or provide social services, people expect those actually extracting natural resources from their area to not only compensate them for negative externalities, but also to take responsibility for local development.[16] Finally, there are more frequent encounters with security forces, both private and state, because of their high numbers in these areas – making these encounters less violent is a main concern of the VPs.

In short, there is a fundamental difference between the MNC position and transnational liberal-economic discourse on security on the one hand, and the perceptions of local communities on the other. Companies use a legal argument rooted in liberal-economic discourse emphasizing their private property rights: Security concerns refer to the protection of their private assets. MNCs are confronted with a social and political environment that poses much more fundamental questions to them than the (narrow) security of their assets: human security that comprises access to and redistribution of benefits from natural resources.

16 Interview with manager community relations and social development, AGA, 3 October 2007, Johannesburg; Kapelus 2006.

Routine security practices

How do AGA and Anvil, who have gained high visibility internationally and do commit to various voluntary initiatives, such as the VPs, address these conflicts and security challenges? The compliance perspective focuses on activities that conform to liberal human rights oriented governance. However, local company agents and contracted state and non-state security forces invoke three sets of security practices. They combine practices of communication, engagement with communities, and reduction in the use of violence with two other strategies: a traditional fortress strategy employing practices of coercion (violence), and a strategy of indirect rule which often reproduces and strengthens unaccountable and repressive state and local non-state political structures. The three sets of security practices are embedded in different discourses and practice fields (Hönke 2010a; forthcoming). The research agenda on non-state actors and governance should consider all three to better understand corporate impact on local security and the limitations of (compliance with) voluntary transnational principles.

The first set of security practices evolves around the logic of fortress protection, and best represents the distinction between companies as private entities and the state as being responsible for issues in the public sphere, as established in liberal political theory. Within this logic of fortress protection, the main strategy of firms is to block themselves off from their environment and thus from theft, small-scale mining and popular protest (Hönke 2010b). Both AGA and Anvil work with private and state security forces to this end.[17] Unlike in South Africa, for instance, companies operating in the DRC have to work with state security forces and intelligence on every mine site, since only state security forces are allowed to carry arms. The mining companies call on special state security forces for robust operations, such as protection against social unrest and armed patrols. In Katanga, some police stations, and in particular the provincial inspectorate of the PNC in Lubumbashi, hold special contingents of the *Police d'Intervention*, which both the firms and the governor can rely on when they feel order is getting out of hand.[18] Anvil, for instance, called in rapid reaction forces of the police to suppress protest by artisanal miners and 'clean' their concession. Having been evicted from the large new concession owned by Freeport McMoRan, about 7000 artisanal miners worked on the riverbanks of the concession of Anvil Mining in Kolwezi. Even though Anvil Mining claims there had been no problems, media reports describe how tensions over plans for eventually evicting miners from the concession led to conflict and police in-

17 Interview with the security managers of Anvil, November 22, 2008, Lubumbashi; also with security manager AGA, 3 April 2007, Johannesburg.

18 Interview with chief of operations, Congolese National Police, provincial head offices in Katanga, 7 November 2008, Lubumbashi.

tervention (Bavier 2008). Private security agents (PSCs) and state security forces, but also fences, barriers, controls and searches in villages, exercise violence and decrease security in the local arena. While the VPs seek to reduce the level of direct, physical violence, they do not address more indirect violence and insecurity beyond direct physical threats.

The second set of corporate security practices revolves around strategies of indirect rule, using personal networks, bribes and paying the state 'as-you-go' (Hönke 2012, Reno 2001). It comprises building relations with key persons in important political networks and positions within the fragmented, personalized and dysfunctional state apparatus, as well as with powerful local authorities such as traditional chiefs. In areas of limited statehood, such as the DRC, the state may seem dysfunctional when compared to the ideal of a modern welfare state with constitutional democracy. This does not necessarily mean that the state is absent. Companies depend on maintaining good relations with agents at all levels of the state apparatus. Security issues in the more narrow sense concern the provincial governor and key figures in the local and provincial police. In order to secure the concession and political support for its operation, a company needs to relate to the power players in government, including the president, Joseph Kabila, and the former minister of mines, today special advisor to the president. Investing in the lucrative Congolese mining sector hardly works without a "political umbrella" (Global Witness 2007: 42ff.). Anvil paid the key brokers of mining deals in Laurent Kabila's AFDL and later in the government by adding them to its board of directors for several years.[19] In Mongbwalu, it was the militia controlling the area, the FNI, to which the local AGA manager felt obliged to pay 8000 $ in 2005 (HRW 2005).

In the DRC, state agents use state office for private gains, and part of the reason for that is that they do not get paid (Hönke 2010a: 228-237). When AGA called in the police for investigating a theft that had occurred on the concession, the police officer asked for 50$ to cover the expenses of getting to the concession and doing his work. After being denied the money, he refused to hand over the results of his investigation – without which AGA could not pursue the case.[20] Such everyday service-by-demand behaviour of state representatives is not an exception from the rule, but rather the norm.[21]

19 Interview with Bill Turner, CEO of Anvil Mining, broadcast of "The Kilwa Incident", Four Corners, Australian Broadcasting Corporation, 6 June 2005.

20 Interview with social relations and community manager, AGA, 3 October 2007, Johannesburg.

21 See for instance the concise statement by DRC expert Timothy Raeymaekers on this topic (Raeymaekers 2009).

Studying local perceptions of (in)security and corporate security practices from the bottom up puts the VPs in context and raises several important issues that should be addressed more systematically and more in depth by research on companies and governance in areas of limited statehood.

First, transnational standards contradict and conflict with local norms that are relevant for the security practices of multinational companies in the extractive industries. Both AGA and Anvil have developed human rights training programmes in compliance with the VPs. Yet, in the DRC, foreign companies are not allowed to get involved in any training of state security forces. Out of historical fear of state capture, and in order to support the new Kabila government and its sovereignty, local, provincial and national police have not agreed to receive any training. Anvil negotiated that the company be allowed to give a briefing on the VPs to the commander in chief of the Congolese police who would then decide how to integrate this into the police training. State officials, in turn, emphasize that they were providing their own training. Yet, it remains well-known that the state security sector barely receives any training at all in this respect (Hönke 2010a: 225-27).[22] Moreover, there are few structural incentives for police agents to change behaviour. Not receiving any salary, police officers usually ask for money and extort revenue from artisanal mining. Those who gained experience in the Mobutu police force or militias during the Congolese wars are used to repressive regime policing.

Companies depend on working with state police and state police services, and thus pay for services such as the enforcement of their contract and their property rights (see the fencing-off strategy) as well as for complying with host state regulation. Seeking to comply with the VPs, AGA and Anvil unavoidably come into conflict with competing norms at the local level, such as the 'politics of the belly' (Bayart 1993; see Hönke 2010a: 182-188, 2012 and forthcoming). Expecting local security agents to behave like agents of a Weberian rational-democratic state does not match the realities in postcolonial states. The norm at the local level is to renumerate state agents and their services in a 'pay-as-you-go' and informal manner, and to provide immediate benefits to people affected by the economic activity. Distribution of revenues through the state rarely takes place. Thus, companies are expected to comply with contradicting norms, the politics of the belly, and the VPs. Sanctions may be more immediate from the locally stronger institutionalised norm. Interesting enough, recent opinion polls in the DRC show that the majority of peo-

22 Interviews with the *Chef des Operations* PNC, *Inspection Provincial de Lubumbashi*, 7 November 2008, Lubumbashi; *Inspecteur et Commandant Police Minière et des Hydro* (PMH), PNC, *Inspection Générale*, November 10 2008, Lubumbashi.

ple want the state, and one reason might be that enough people manage to get private gains out of it.[23]

The second reason to integrate our bottom-up approach into the research landscape lies in its ability to bring into view unintended effects on local communities. Compliance research asks whether the Voluntary Principles are adopted and effectively implemented. Such an approach dismisses the important – often unintended – effects that transnational standards may have. One revolves around the indirect strengthening of unaccountable state institutions. The other revolves around shifts in security, power and increased conflict within communities (see Hönke, with Thomas 2012).

The managerial approach of the VPs, emphasizing risk assessment, awareness raising, communication, and training, neglects the material and discursive context in which local company and state agents work. State security forces are financed through individuals using their position within the state to pursue private goals. Clientelism and corruption are organising principles of local polities and the Congolese state. This is a long-established social system. Working with the state and its security forces inevitably leads to reproducing that apparatus, which in turn may facilitate extortion and human rights abuses. Companies such as Anvil in the DRC emphasize now that they were providing neither money nor fuel to local police officers – but doubts about how that may have worked in practice remain (see also the example of AGA and the police officer above).

As shown by our top-down compliance analysis of Anvil and AGA, transnational norms have strengthened proactive engagement with communities and security forces through communication and development initiatives with the former, and training with the latter. Both Anvil and AGA work with Pact Congo, which has set up forums in the communities living adjacent to extraction sites, in which issues of concern may be discussed and people are supposed to participate in decisions regarding social investments.[24] While more in-depth research is required to study the functions and effects of these new structures, it can be assumed that they provide new means of managing security risks by co-opting those who may cause trouble, such as in the Niger Delta. Yet, participatory structures at village level, such as elected development committees deciding on the allocation of company development money within a community, often come into conflict with pre-existing local power structures and competition over influence and resources. While future field work will provide the basis for examining these points in relation to AGA and Anvil in the DRC, examples from other areas demonstrate how much the corporate

23 Interviews with the *Chef des Operations* PNC, *Inspection Provincial de Lubumbashi*, 7 November 2008, Lubumbashi; *Inspecteur et Commandant Police Minière et des Hydro* (PMH), PNC, *Inspection Générale*, November 10 2008, Lubumbashi.

24 Interview with social development manager, Anvil Mining, November 2008, Lubumbashi; Interview with conflict and human rights branch, Pact Congo, October 2008, Lubumbashi.

need for stability, on the one hand, and requirements for participatory approaches by transnational standards, on the other hand, may conflict with each other (Geenen and Hönke forthcoming; Hönke 2012). Companies seem to have a tendency to work with powerful actors in the local arena who are able to provide contract security because of their legal entitlement to land – chiefs with land rights recognised by the law, such as in South Africa – thereby sidelining other groups and opinions at the local level (see Welker 2009).

Overall, colonialism, previous extraction from the area, patterns of indirect rule, and the clientele position of the DRC vis-à-vis the US and other Western countries turned the Congolese state into a "shadow state" (Reno 1995). State representatives use their status to get paid by the population – and by companies. As a result, mining companies are subject to competing norms. By also playing by the rules of the game of a 'politics of the belly', the companies systematically reproduce autocratic and corrupt polities in the DRC through their payments in bribes and taxes, through legitimizing these regimes and enlisting their sovereignty (Reno 1998; Reno 2001; also Hönke 2010b and 2012), and through their local governance practices.

5. Conclusion

The Voluntary Principles have gained importance for MNCs. Respecting human rights has become part of a global script, which is codified in a growing number of transnational institutions seeking to keep MNCs socially responsible. MNCs, in turn, increasingly commit themselves to the transnational norms and rules, partly because their practices have become subject to public scrutiny and criticism. The naming and shaming by transnational NGOs also helps to make companies honour their commitments. Our case studies of AngloGold Ashanti and Anvil Mining in the period 2007 to 2010 testify to the efforts of companies to become more sensitive to human rights issues while securing their assets in zones of weak governance and conflict.

From a top-down perspective, which takes voluntary standards as a starting point and evaluates corporate compliance with them, MNCs have been making at least partial progress, particularly on the output side. AGA and Anvil have incorporated the VPs into their corporate policies and management systems. They have also changed their security practices engaging in communication with local communities and in human rights training for public and private security forces.

Yet, we also find serious problems of non-compliance. Our bottom-up approach, taking the full range of company security practices into perspective, reveals systemic limits of the VPs, which go far beyond vaguely defined performance criteria, weak enforcement mechanisms, and a narrow membership base. Companies' communication and participation structures with communities lack autonomy from the company and are seldom representative of all groups in the areas affected by mining. Protecting company assets through fencing off and deterrence with the help of state security forces and PSCs is complicity in violence. There is a very thin line between working with state security forces in particular and not supporting extortion and repression by them. Human rights training to police deployed on site does not take place.

Making efforts to implement the VPs, MNC remain profit-oriented. They are not turned away by hostile environments afflicted by insecurity, corruption, and human rights violations (UNCTAD 2007). Although the World Bank lists the DRC as one of the worst countries to do business in (World Bank 2008), it has received high international mining investments since 2004. Companies' priority of doing business implies acceptance of conflicts over access to land and relocation, as well as other issues related to who has to bear the costs of mining and proper compensation. Issues of (re)distribution of wealth and access to resources are not addressed by the VPs. Property rights raise serious issues about the legitimacy of contractual relations between the MNCs and governments. In fact, one may argue that the VPs help MNCs avoid such issues by deflecting public pressure and allowing them to continue operations, thereby sustaining existing political regimes and economic structures (Hönke 2010b, forthcoming; Reno 2001).

Our findings, hence, go beyond the classical bottom-up approach we know from implementation studies and which also emphasizes practices and conflicts at the local that undermine compliance. Rather than merely focusing on the decoupling of formal institutions and behavioural practices, we demonstrate that MNC are subject to competing rationalities that often render compliance difficult. In addition and somewhat paradoxically, MNC may use voluntary standards to duck compliance. These findings have some important policy implications.

The effectiveness of the VPs can certainly be improved by giving them more teeth, e.g. by making their rules more precise, by stepping up monitoring and sanctioning procedures, or by placing MNCs under (more) NGO scrutiny. The recent take-over of Anvil Mining by a major Chinese company underlines, in addition, that it is important to create inclusive institutions of global governance. In the field of mining and security this means that at the least actors from China, India and Brazil need to be involved in creating and implementing regulatory initiatives in order to make these initiatives relevant and effective. Conflicts over property rights and the (re)distribution of economic and political resources, however, will not be solved by the prevailing managerial approach to the governance of business and human rights. If the VPs do not account for the political rationalities and competing norms of the local and transnational context in which MNCs do business, their effectiveness is likely to remain limited. Our bottom-up approach thus points to serious limitations of transnational voluntary programs such as the VPs. They ignore the global political economy of mining in which MNCs, home and host state governments, transnational expert communities and non-state actors not only push for softer regulation, but also tend to sustain inequality in access to natural resources and welfare.

Finally, other important issues emerge in a bottom-up (re)evaluation of corporate security practices and their effects on local collective security and human rights. A major concern is the question of how inclusive corporate contributions are to security governance. Cui bono? Do companies provide security as a private or club good, or do companies aspire to extend their reach to the entire community surrounding their production site? And even if they do, what are the effects of corporate security governance on neighbouring communities, i.e. to what extent does the security of one community simply shift the problem to another?

6. Literature

Primary documents

AngloGold Ashanti (AGA) 2005: Human Rights Report on AngloGold Ashanti's Activities in the DRC (news release 1 July 2005), in: http://www.anglogold.co.za/NR/rdonlyres/1BC8B7B3-6363-48B3-AE85-B315606CF248/0/2005Jun01_SAreleaseDRC.pdf; 31 July 2010.

AngloGold Ashanti (AGA) 2008: Submission to the Voluntary Principles on Security and Human Rights Plenary (March 2008), in: http://www.anglogold.com/NR/rdonlyres/E29B8879-3F6E-43A6-BC5F-E5B46E1EF703/0/VoluntaryPrinciplesFinalReport2008Plenary.pdf; 1 August 2010.

AngloGold Ashanti (AGA) 2009a: AngloGold Ashanti Annual Financial Statements 2009.Corporate Profile: A truly global producer, in: http://www.anglogold.com/subwebs/InformationForInvestors/Reports09/AnnualReport09/profile.htm; 5 August 2010.

AngloGold Ashanti (AGA) 2009b: Submission to the Voluntary Principles on Security and Human Rights Plenary (March 2009), in: http://anglogoldashanti.com.au/subwebs/InformationForInvestors/Reports08/AGA-VPHRS.pdf; 2 August 2010.

AngloGold Ashanti (AGA) 2009c: AngloGold Ashanti Sustainability Review: Supplementary Information 2009. Social Performance: Human Rights, in: http://www.anglogoldashanti.co.za/subwebs/informationforinvestors/reports09/SustainabilityReview09/gri_humanrights.htm; 31 July 2010.

AngloGold Ashanti (AGA) 2009d: AngloGold Ashanti Sustainability Review 2009 Environment, Community and Human Rights, in: http://www.anglogoldashanti.co.za/subwebs/informationforinvestors/reports09/SustainabilityReview09/environment.htm; 31 July 2010.

AngloGoldAshanti (AGA) a, in: http://www.anglogold.com/NR/rdonlyres/C428E0C4-0F0C-4062-BC32-E7D1C9790F32/0/VoluntaryPrinciples2009reportFebruary2010_postauditFinalversion12March.pdf; 1 August.8. 2010 (year of publication not given).

AngloGoldAshanti (AGA) b, in: http://www.anglogold.com/Sustainability/AngloGold+Ashanti+and+the+Voluntary+Principles.htm; 31 July 2010 (year of publication not given).

Anvil Mining 2007: Code of Business Conduct (September 2007), in: http://www.anvilmining.com/files/AVM%20CP01%20Anvil%20Code%20of%20Business%2Conduct%20(vA17290).pdf; 2 August 2010.

Anvil Mining 2008a: Anvil Mining Annual Information Form 2008 (28.3.2008), in: http://www.anvilmining.com/files/AIF_2008__clean_FINAL2.pdf; 5 August 2010.

Anvil Mining 2008b: The Voluntary Principles on Security and Human Rights. Working Paper July 2008, World Bank Group/MIGA, Washington, DC.

Anvil Mining 2009: Anvil Mining Annual Information Form 2009 (31 March 2009), in: http://www.anvilmining.com/files/Anvil-AIF-2009.pdf; 5 August 2010.

Anvil Mining 2010: Anvil Divests its Interest in the Dikulushi Tenements in the DRCand Updates Construction Progress at Kinsevere Stage II (News Release 26 February 2010), in: http://www.anvilmining.com/files/20100225%20Divestment%20of%20Interest%20in%20AMC%20&%20KSII%20Update.pdf; 10 August 2010.

Anvil Mining 2011: Corporate Structure, in: http://www.anvilmining.com/go/corporate/corporate-structure; 28 March 2011.

Secondary literature

Anton, Wilma Rose Q., George Deltas, and Madhu Khanna. 2004. Incentives for Environmental Self-Regulation and Implications for Environmental Performance. Journal of Environmental Economics and Management 48 (1):632-654.

Auld, Graeme, Steven Bernstein, and Benjamin Cashore. 2008. The New Corporate Social Responsibility. *Annual Review of Environment and Resources* 33:413-435.

Bansal, Pratima, and Kendall Roth. 2000. Why Companies Go Green: A Model of Ecological Responsiveness. *Academy of Management Journal* 43 (4):717-736.

Barney, Jay B. 1997. *Gaining and Sustaining Competitive Advantage*. Reading, MA: Addison-Wesley.

Baron, David P. 2003. Private Politics. *Journal of Economics and Management* 12 (1):31-66.

Bavier, Joe 2008: Police Clash with Miners in Congo Copper Heartland (Reuters 31 March 2008), in: http://www.reuters.com/article/latestCrisis/idUSL31912922; 23 June 2009.

Bayart, Jean-François 1993. *The State in Africa: Politics of the Belly*. London und New York: Longman.

Bhagwati, Jagdish, and Robert Hudec. 1996. *Fair Trade and Harmonization. Prerequisites for Free Trade?* Cambridge, MA: MIT Press.

Blanton, Robert G., and Shannon Lindsey Blanton. 2007. Human Rights and Trade: Beyond the "Spotlight". *International Interactions* 33 (2):97-117.

Börzel, Tanja A. 2010. Governance with(out) Government – False Promises or Flawed Premises. *SFB Working Papers; Sonderforschungsbereich 700, Freie Universität Berlin* (23).

Börzel, Tanja A., and Thomas Risse. 2010. Governance without a State – Can it Work? *Regulation and Governance* 4 (2):1-22.

Börzel, Tanja A., Adrienne Héritier, Nicole Kranz, and Christian Thauer. 2011. Racing to the Top? Regulatory Competition among Firms in Areas of Limited Statehood. In *Governance without a State? Policies and Politics in Areas of Limited Statehood*, edited by T. Risse. New York: Columbia University Press.

Börzel, Tanja A., and Christian Thauer, eds. forthcoming. *Racing to the Top? Business and Governance in South Africa*. London: Palgrave.

Bowen, Frances, Aloysius Newenham-Kahindi, and Irene Herremans. 2008. *Engaging the Community: A Systematic Review*. Calgary: University of Calgary.

Brühl, Tanja. 2007. Public-private partnerships: unlike partners? Assessing New Forms of Regulation. In *Globalization. State of the Art and Perspectives*, edited by S. A. Schirm. London: Routledge.

Deitelhoff, Nicole, and Klaus-Dieter Wolf, eds. 2010. *Corporate Security Responsibility? Corporate Governance Contributions to Peace and Security in Zones of Conflict*. Houndmills: Palgrave.

Epstein, Marc J. 2008. *Making Sustainability Work. Best Practices in Managing and Measuring Corporate Social, Environmental and Economic Impacts*. Sheffield: Greenleaf Publishing.

Eweje, Gabriel. 2005. The Role of MNEs in Community Development Initiatives in Developing Countries. Corporate Social Responsibility at Work in Nigeria and South Africa. *Business and Society* 45 (2):93-129.

Flohr, Annegret, Lothar Rieth, Sandra Schwindenhammer, and Klaus Dieter Wolf. 2010. *The Role of Business in Global Governance. Corporations as Norm-Entrepreneurs*. Basingstoke: Palgrave.

Freeman, Benett. 2005. To What Extent Can Voluntarism Provide Answers? In *Wilton Park Conference on Business and Human Rights: advancing the agenda*.

Freeman, Bennett. 2002. The Voluntary Principles on Security and Human Rights. In *Case Studies of Multistakeholder Partnerships*, edited by V. Haufler. New York: UN Global Compact Office.

Freeman, Bennett, and Genoveva Hernandez Uriz. 2003. Managing Risk and Building Trust. The Challenge of Implementing the Voluntary Principles on Security and Human Rights. In *Business and Human Rights. Dilemmas and Solutions*, edited by R. Sullivan. Sheffield: Greenleaf Publishing.

Frynas, Jedrzej George. 2000. *Oil in Nigeria: Conflict and Litigation Between Oil Companies and Village Communities*. Hamburg: Lit Verlag.

Garcia-Johnson, Ronnie. 2000. *Exporting Environmentalism*. Cambridge: MIT Press.

Global Witness. 2007. Oil and Mining in Violent Places: Why voluntary codes for companies don't guarantee human rights. London: Global Witness.

Geenen, Sara, Kamundala, Gabriel and Iragi, Francine. 2011. Le pari qui paralysait. La suspension des activités minières artisanales au Sud-Kivu. *L'Afrique des Grands Lacs. Annuaire 2010-2011.* Paris: L'Harmattan.

Geenen, Sara and Hönke, Jana forthcoming. 'Land grabbing' by mining companies. State reconfiguration and local contentions in South-Kivu, DRC. In A. Ansom (ed.) *'Land Grabbing' in the Great Lakes Region of Africa.* Basingstoke: Palgrave.

Hamann, Ralph, Peresha Sinha, Farai Kopfudzaruwa, and Christoph Schild. 2009. Business and Human Rights in South Africa: An Analysis of Antecendents of Human Rights Due Diligence. *Journal of Business Ethics* (87):453-473.

Hansen, Thomas H. 2009. Governing the Extractive Indutries: The Extractive Industries Transparency Initiative and the Voluntary Principles on Security and Human Rights. In *ISA Annual Convention 2009*. New York.

Haufler, Virginia. 2001. *A Pulic Role for the Private Sector – Industry Self-Regulation in a Global Economy*. Washington D.C.: Carnegie Endowment for International Peace.

Hendry, Jamie. 2006. Taking Aim at Business. *Business and Society* 45 (1):47-86.

Héritier, Adrienne, and Dirk Lehmkuhl, eds. 2008. *The Shadow of Hierarchy and New Modes of Governance. Special Issue Journal of Public Policy, Vol. 28 (1).*

Hill, Michael, and Peter L. Hupe. 2002. *Implementing Public Policy. Governance in Theory and Practice*. London: Sage.

Hofferberth, Matthias. 2010. The Binding Dynamics of Non-Binding Governance Arrangements. In *ISA Annual Convention 2010*. New Orleans.

Hönke, Jana. 2010a. Liberal Discourse and Hybrid Practise in Transnational Security Governance: Companies in Congo and South Africa in the 19th and 21st Centuries, Freie Universität Berlin.

Hönke, Jana. 2010b. New political topographies. Mining companies and indirect discharge in Southern Katanga (DRC). *Politique Africaine* 120, 105-128.

Hönke, Jana 2012. Multinationals and Security Governance in the Community. Participation, discipline and indirect rule. *Journal of Intervention and Statebuilding,* 6 (1)**,** 89-105.

Hönke, Jana. forthcoming. *Transnational Companies and Security Governance. Securing Business Spaces*. London: Routledge.

Hönke, Jana, with Esther Thomas. 2012. *Governance for whom? Inclusiveness, indirect effects and externalities*. SFB Working Papers; Sonderforschungsbereich 700, Freie Universität Berlin (31).

Hönke, Jana and Nicole Kranz forthcoming: Cleaning up their act, or more? Mining companies and environmental protection in South Africa. In Börzel, Tanja A. and Thauer, Christian (eds.). *Business and Governance in South Africa.* Palgrave.

Höppner, Ulrike, and Dominik Nagl. 2008. Jenseits der Staatlichkeit: Governance und Gouvernementalität als postmoderne Konzepte des Regierens. In *Transdisziplinäre Governanceforschung. Gemeinsam hinter den Staat blicken*, edited by S. De La Rosa, U. Höppner and M. Kötter. Baden-Baden: Nomos.

HRW. 2005. The curse of gold (Democratic Republic of Congo). New York: Human Rights Watch.

Jim Freedman Consulting. 2006. OECD Audit of Anvil Mining Limited. Katanga Province, Democratic Republic of Congo.

Johnston, Les, and Clifford Shearing. 2003. *Governing Security*. London / New York: Routledge.

Kapelus, Paul. 2006. Anglo Gold Ashanti in the Democratic Republic of Congo: Management Challenges and Responses to Operating in a Weak Governance Area. edited by U. G. C. L. Forum. New York, NY: UN Global Compact.

Kapelus, Paul, Ralph Hamann, and Ed O'Keefe. 2008. Learning from the Experience of AngoGold Ashanti in the DRC. In *The Business of Sustainable Development in Africa: Human Rights, Partnerships, Alternative Business Models*, edited by R. Hamann, S. Woolman and C. Sprague. Pretoria: UNU Press.

Kolk, Ans, Rob van Tulder, and Carlijn Welters. 2005. Setting New Global Rules? TNCs and Codes of Conduct. *Transnational Corporations* 14 (3):1-28.

Kollman, Kelley, and Aseem Prakash. 2001. Green by Choice? Cross-National Variations in Firms' Responses to EMS-Based Environmental Regimes. *World Politics* 53 (April 2001): 399-430.

Ladwig, Bernd, and Beate Rudolf. 2011. International Legal and Moral Standards of Good Governance in Fragile States. In *Governance in Areas of Limited Statehood*, edited by T. Risse and U. Lehmkuhl. New York: Columbia University Press.

Leander, Anna. 2010. Practices Providing Order: The Private Military/Security Business and Global (in)Security Governance. In *Business and Global Governance – Business in Global Governance* edited by M. Ougaard and A. Leander. London: Routledge.

Lofdahl, Corey L. 2002. *Environmental Impact of Globalization and Trade. A Systems Study*. Cambridge, MA: MIT Press.

Lund-Thomson, Peter. 2005. Corporate Accountability in South Africa. The Role of Community Mobilizing in Environmental Governance. *International Affairs* 81 (3):619-633.

Mayntz, Renate, and Fritz W. Scharpf. 1995a. Der Ansatz des akteurszentrierten Institutionalismus. In *Gesellschaftliche Selbstregulierung und politische Steuerung*, edited by R. Mayntz and F. W. Scharpf. Frankfurt a.M.: Campus.

Mayntz, Renate, and Fritz W. Scharpf. 1995b. Steuerung und Selbstorganisation in staatsnahen Sektoren. In *Gesellschaftliche Selbstregulierung und politische Steuerung*, edited by R. Mayntz and F. W. Scharpf. Frankfurt; New York: Campus.

Mol, Arthur P. J. 2001. *Globalization and Environmental Reforms: The Ecological Modernization of the Global Economy*. Cambridge, MA: MIT Press.

Muchlinski, Peter T. 2007. *Multinational Enterprises and the Law, The Oxford international law library*. Oxford: Oxford Univ. Press.

Murphy, Dale. 2000. *The Structure of Regulatory Competition: Corporations and Public Policies in a Global Economy*. Oxford: Oxford University Press.

Newell, Peter J. 2001. Managing Multinationals. The Governance of Investment for the Environment. *Journal of International Development* 13 (7):907-919.

Parker, Christine. 2002. *The Open Corporation: Effective Self-regulation and Democracy*. Cambridge: Cambridge University Press.

Porter, Michael E., and Mark R. Kramer. 2002. The Competitive Advantage of Corporate Philanthropy. *Harvard Business Review* 80 (12):56-68.

Porter, Michael E., and Claas van der Linde. 1995. Toward a New Conception of the Environment-Competitiveness Relationship. *Journal of Economic Perspectives* 9 (4):97-118.

Potoski, Matthew, and Aseem Prakash. 2005. Green Clubs and Voluntary Governance: ISO 14001 and Firms' Regulatory Compliance. *American Journal of Political Science* 49 (2):235-248.

Potoski, Matthew, and Aseem Prakash. 2006. Racing to the Bottom? Trade, Environmental Governance, and ISO 14001. *American Journal of Political Science* 50 (2):350-364.

Prakash, Aseem, and Matthew Potoski. 2006. *The Voluntary Environmentalists: Green Clubs, ISO 14001 and Voluntary Environmental Regulations*. Cambridge: Cambridge University Press.

Prakash, Sethi. 2005. The Effectiveness of Industry-Based Codes in Serving Public Interest. The Case of the International Council on Mining and Metals. *Transnational Corporations* 14 (3): 55-100.

Pressman, Jeffrey L., and Aaron Wildavsky. 1984. *Implementation. How Great Expectations in Washington are Dashed in Oakland.* 2 ed. Berkeley: University of California Press.

Raustiala, Kal, and Anne Marie Slaughter. 2002. International Law, International Relations and Compliance. In *Handbook of International Relations*, edited by W. Carlsnaes, T. Risse and B. A. Simmons. London: Sage Publications.

Reno, William. 2001. How Sovereignty Matters: International Markets and the Political Economy of Local Politics in Weak States. In *Intervention & Transnationalism in Africa: Global-Local Networks of Power*, edited by T. M. Callaghy, R. Kassimir and R. Latham. Cambridge: Cambridge University Press.

Reno, William S. K. 1998. Mines, Money, and the Problem of State-Building in Congo. *Issue: A Journal of Opinion* 26 (1):14-17.

Reno, William 1995. *Corruption and State Politics in Sierra Leone.* Cambridge: Cambridge University Press.

Risse, Thomas, Stephen Ropp, and Kathryn Sikkink, eds. forthcoming. *From Commitment to Compliance. The Persistent Power of Human Rights*. Cambridge: Cambridge University Press.

Ronit, Carsten, and Volker Schneider, eds. 2000. *Private Organizations in Global Politics*. London: Routledge.

Ruggie, John G. 2004. How to Marry Civic Politics and Private Governance. In *The Impact of Global Corporations on Global Governance*, edited by C. C. o. E. a. I. Affairs. New York: Carnegie Council on Ethics and International Affairs.

Ruggie, John G. 2007. Business and Human Rights: Mapping International Standards of Responsibility and Accountability for Corporate Acts. Report of the Special Representative of the Secretary-General on the Issue of Human Rights and Transnational Corporations and Other Business Enterprises. New York: U.N..

Ruggie, John G. 2008. Protect, Respect and Remedy: A Framework for Business and Human Rights. Report of the Special Representative of the Secretary-General on the Issue of Human Rights and Transnational Corporations and Other Business Enterprises. New York: U.N.

Ruggie, John G. 2010. Remarks at Mid-Year Special Session Voluntary Principles on Security and Human Rights. U.S. Department of State Washington D.C.

Schäferhoff, Marco, Sabine Campe, and Christopher Kaan. 2009. Transnational Public-Private Partnerships in International Relations: Making Sense of Concepts, Research Frameworks, and Results. *International Studies Review* 11 (3):451-474.

Schepers, Donald.H. 2006. The Impact of NGO Network Conflict on the Corporate Social Responsibility Strategies of Multinational Corporations. *Business and Society* 45 (3):282-299.

Smith, C N. 2008. Consumers as Drivers of Corporate Social Responsibility. In *The Oxford Handbook of Corporate Social Responsibility*, edited by A. Crane, A. McWilliams, D. Matten, J. Moon and D. S. Siegel. Oxford: Oxford University Press.

Spar, Deborah L., and Lane T. LaMure. 2003. The Power of Activism: Assessing the Impact of NGOs on Global Business. *California Management Review* 45:78-101.

Szablowski, David. 2007. *Transnational Law and Local Struggles: Mining Communities and the World Bank*. Oxford: Oxford University Press.

Thauer, Christian R. 2010. Corporate Social Responsibility in the Regulatory Void – Does the Promise Hold? Self-Regulation by Business in South Africa and China. PhD Thesis, Social and Political Science Department, European University Institute, Florence.

Thauer, Christian R. 2012. Goodness Comes From Within. Intra-organizational Dynamics of Corporate Social Responsibility. *Business and Society*.

UNCTAD. 2007. World Investment Report: Transnational Corporations, Extractive Industries and Development. New York, Geneva.

Vogel, David, and Robert Kagan, eds. 2004. *Dynamics of Regulatory Change: How Globalization Affects National Regulatory Policies*. Berkeley, Los Angeles: University of California Press.

Waygood, Steve. 2006. *Capital Market Campaigning. The Impact of NGOs on Companies, Shareholder Value and Reputational Risk*. London: Risk Books.

Wheeler, David. 2001. Racing to the Bottom? Foreign Investment and Air Pollution in Developing Countries. *Journal of Environment and Development* 10 (3):225-245.

World Bank. 2008. Doing Business 2008. edited by World Bank. Washington, DC: World Bank.

Zalik, Anna. 2004. The Niger Delta: 'Petro Violence' and 'Partnership Development'. *Review of African Political Economy* (101):401-424.

Zerk, Jennifer. 2006. *Multinationals and Corporate Social Responsibility*. Cambridge: Cambridge University Press.

Zeitfracht Medien GmbH
Ferdinand-Jühlke-Straße 7
99095 Erfurt, Deutschland
produktsicherheit@kolibri360.de